Promise
Introduction

   Most of the pictures in this collection are accompanied by stories. Why stories?

   Think of all your experience with family, friends and acquaintances at home, in work and in play; all the activities, the good times and the hard times of daily life. Imagine this as a long horizontal line — like the field in our picture. Now imagine the healing, redemptive power of God's love as a constant vertical descending line. Where these two lines intersect — where they form a cross — there is always a story. Theories, philosophical arguments and abstractions can interest us. They often have great value, providing stimulating insights, coherence and a point of reference. But it is the story that moves us. It is the story that we live.

   In the beginning of his First Letter, John refers to his relationship with Jesus: "I am writing to you about something I have heard, something I have seen with my own eyes, and touched with my own hands" (I John 1-4). These sound like the words of someone with a story to tell. He goes on to say, "I share this with you, that our joy may be complete."

   So — I read, contemplate, and wonder about Scripture. And on those occasions when a Scripture's meaning seems revealed in some parable of daily experience, then to share what I have glimpsed brings – as the apostle says — "Joy."

   On this design, it was especially satisfying to add "promise becomes reality." Combined with the very familiar Christmas reading from the Gospel of Luke, those three words penetrate the familiarity, going directly to the deepest meaning of Luke's message. The prophecy has been fulfilled. The promise comes true. Our Savior is here.

AND, THERE WERE SHEPHERDS ABIDING IN THE FIELD, KEEPING WATCH OVER THEIR FLOCKS AT NIGHT. AND, LO, THE ANGEL OF THE LORD CAME UPON THEM, AND THE GLORY OF THE LORD SHONE ROUND ABOUT THEM; AND THEY WERE SORE AFRAID. BUT THE ANGEL SAID UNTO THEM "FEAR NOT: FOR, BEHOLD, I BRING YOU GOOD TIDINGS OF GREAT JOY, WHICH SHALL BE TO ALL PEOPLE. FOR UNTO YOU IS BORN THIS DAY IN THE CITY OF DAVID, A SAVIOUR, WHICH IS CHRIST THE LORD." FROM THE GOSPEL OF LUKE, CHAPTER 2: VERSES 8-11

...promise becomes reality.

1

Acknowledgments

In the creation of this book, I received generous help and guidance from: George Beahm, Mary Beahm, Joshua Podesta, Alexander Podesta, Nan Powlinson, David Powlinson, and Rick Hoyt.

My gratitude to them is boundless.

Summer 2005

Published in Williamsburg, Virginia. Printed in China by Palace Press International.

ISBN 1-893914-07-0
First Edition

J O Y

DESIGN AND COMMENTARY

IN THY PRESENCE IS JOY.   PSALM 16:11

MICHAEL PODESTA

Contents

26
MESSENGERS –
VARYING AND
UNVARYING IN
FORM AND COLOR
AND RHYTHM –
COMBINING AND
RECOMBINING
IN INK AND LIGHT –
MOVING ACROSS
PAPER, MARBLE,
METAL, COTTON,
WOOD, AND AIR –
ALL BECAUSE
THERE IS
SOMETHING
YOU
HAVE TO
TELL ME –
SOMETHING I
HAVE TO
TELL YOU.

MICHAEL

26 Messengers
Communication

THE PROMOTER of an arts and crafts show I planned to participate in called with a novel idea. "I would like all you exhibitors to write a little statement, just a paragraph or two, in which you share with the public your personal philosophy about your particular art or craft. What do you say?" I said, "OK."

Potters would be sharing their thoughts about clay, weavers about wool and linen and other fibers, jewelers about precious metals and stones. I obviously needed to say something about the alphabet. These were my words.

The calligraphy on the text was an experiment for me. It is based on letter forms created by the graphic designer Friedrich Neugebauer.

God is Good
Fundamentals

Well, He is.

Joy
Response, Responsibility

ELIZABETH ELLIOT GIVES a wonderful definition of the word "joy." She says, "Joy is not the absence of trouble; it is the presence of God."

I was visiting a friend, a minister in Marietta, Georgia. He was my host while I was at a local arts and crafts show. After dismantling and loading up my exhibit on the final day, Sunday, I returned to his home quite late. There was a note saying he had gone to bed, but that we should get together in the morning for breakfast. When I got up he said, "Let's go out. The phone has been ringing off the hook. This is supposed to be my day off. It's got to be more peaceful at a restaurant."

We talked as we ate. We had each had a hectic Sunday. It's a pattern. We are both very busy. He has a large congregation. I travel to shows twice a month or more. We both have families. Obligations abound.

Predictably, the conversation turned to observance of the Sabbath, to the familiar scriptures about a special day of rest, and so forth. We spoke – a little wistfully, a little guiltily I guess – about the delights of outdoor recreation. For example, my friend loves to sail. We agreed that, beyond the physical exhilaration, there is a rejoicing in nature, barely one step removed from worship.

Over a third cup of coffee I decided to share a trifling – probably presumptuous – little whimsy. I imagine I have reached the afterlife. I am confronted by my Creator. A retrospective ensues. The atmosphere is friendly. My family, my work, the constant activity, and everything else are on clear display. (Perhaps this history appears on a screen, like a movie?) At some point, God turns from the spectacle. In a gesture that seems patient, but maybe a little weary, He brushes His palm across His brow. He looks at me, sighs and says, "Hmmm. Well, it is interesting, I suppose. But, you know Michael, there are certain things we're seeing that are not exactly what I had in mind. We have plenty of time, and there are other matters I would like us to talk about, but before we go any further, there is something I just have to ask you. I know it's only a little detail, but it really puzzles Me. I see where, in your early thirties, you practically stopped, well . . . swimming. You used to love to swim. I created oceans and lakes and rivers for many reasons, of course: an ideal environment for the fish, regulating the weather, regattas, hydroelectric dams, not to mention maritime commerce and drinking water. But one of the main reasons was that I knew swimming would give you joy. That was one of My gifts to you. But then, as we have seen, you just quit. Now," He says this ever so

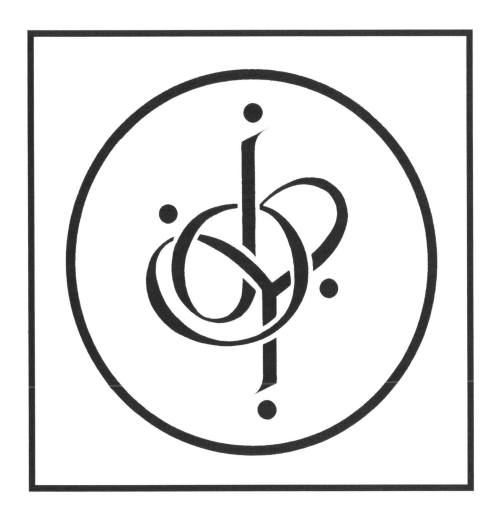

gently, "that's something I would like you to explain to Me."

As we leave the restaurant, I tell my friend that the fantasy stops there because I have reached an impasse. I just can't imagine what to say.

I was reminded of this conversation a couple of weeks later when, at another show, a lady asked me if I had heard of a certain text. She thought it was from the Talmud. She didn't know it word for word, she said, but in effect, it was that, on the Day of Judgment, we will be called to account for, among other things, the gifts we were given to enjoy but would not.

The Psalms tell us, "Let the heavens rejoice and let the earth be glad" and "Delight yourself in the Lord" and "Serve the Lord with gladness." The Shorter Catechism says, "the chief end of man is to glorify God, and to enjoy Him forever."

My hopeless defense before God might be that I give up joy because of responsibilities. The reality turns out to be that joy is a response God expects of me. Joy – so conducive to praise – is a responsibility.

For I Am Persuaded

Vocation

THE GERMAN graphic designer Rudolph Koch once wrote, "The scribe is the servant of the text." In my work, I attempt to serve other people's words through calligraphy and design.

When exhibiting my work, I am often asked, "How did you get started doing this?" The following story gives one answer.

Years ago I was lettering a wall menu for a friend who was getting ready to open a sandwich shop. I had just finished one of the menu items when everyone else involved in the project – plumbers, painters, electricians, all friends of mine – stopped for a morning break. Looking around for something to read while I drank my coffee, I picked up someone's pocket New Testament. At random, I came across Paul's letter to the Romans. "For I am persuaded that neither death nor life... nor angels nor principalities nor powers ... nor any other creature shall be able to separate us from the love of God."

I looked at the careful lettering I had just completed on the wall behind the counter: "Blueberry muffins with cream cheese — 45¢." Somehow, it didn't quite compare. Since the setting was a restaurant, perhaps I can be pardoned for mentioning "a fork in the road."

I finished my work on the menu. But something in me had definitely changed. I found myself yearning to use the alphabet to share a message like Saint Paul's.

For I am
persuaded that
neither death, nor life,
nor angels, nor principalities, nor powers,
nor things present, nor things to come—
nor height, nor depth,
nor any other creature—
shall be able to separate

from the love of US GOD

which is
in our Lord Christ Jesus ✢
Romans, chapter eight, verses thirty-eight
and thirty-nine—

Christ Is

Commitment

In Luke 9:57 a man approaches Jesus, saying, "Master, I will follow You wherever You go."

Jesus answers something like this, "Are you sure? Think about it. Even foxes have dens, birds have their nests, but the Son of Man has nowhere to lay His head." In the Living Bible translation, Jesus "has no earthly home at all."

Christ's path, as we know, was one of daily service and sacrifice. Imagine, "No earthly home at all." But the particular sacrifice He is referring to here seems to me profoundly touching, enough to make me imagine a situation where I am opening my life to Him, and, in hospitality, saying spontaneously, "Well, why don't You come to my house. Stay with me and my family. You're more than welcome." And, no doubt, He would say something like, "You want Me in your life?"

And then, since He knows me better than I know myself, He would add, pointedly, "Are you sure?"

I need to get that room ready, and I need to keep it ready. And while I'm doing that, keep in mind His words from Matthew 25:40, "Inasmuch as ye have done it unto one of the least of these My brethren, ye have done it unto Me."

Christ is the head

of this house

the chosen guest

at every meal

the silent listener

to every conversation.

Heart in God

Accept No Substitutes

MY FRIEND MELISSA'S CAR was in the shop. She didn't want to talk about it. Turns out, the previous Saturday her youngest son — six years old, "into everything," as the saying goes — and a couple of his little buddies were playing in the garage because it was raining. Not only were they playing in the garage, they were playing "Garage," that is, they were pretending to be mechanics, servicing Mom's car. Imaginary substitution is always at the crux of this kind of play. When I was a young boy, a cowboy in my mind's eye, cola diluted to the right color became whiskey; a thumb and perpendicular forefinger made a six-shooter.

For Melissa's son that morning, a can of Fix-a-Flat became a gasoline pump.

"You mean the whole fuel system, carburetor and everything, had to be replaced?" I asked. "Yep," she said grimly.

The engine was only designed to run on gasoline. Our hearts were designed for God. Nothing else works.

You have made us for yourself Almighty God. and our hearts are restless until they rest in You

SAINT AUGUSTINE

Micah

Compassion

THE PROPHET MICAH is evidently addressing a community with very little social conscience. He confronts them aggressively. "Do you think that you can get away with treating other people any way you want, and then just turn around and offer the Lord some elaborate sacrifice — precious oil, fine grain, blood of bulls and goats — and everything is going to be alright? Do you think He's blind? No. He wants you to begin to show compassion. Wake up to the suffering your violent, selfish lifestyle causes in the lives of others. The Lord says it's time you start caring for your neighbor. Offer him a helping hand. And not only does the Lord want you to look out for your neighbor, He wants you to look up to Him."

Micah's brief book moves from condemnation to generous consolation and hope. "He delights in mercy. He will again have compassion on us" (Micah 7:18-19).

That is the relationship, then, in which we will all be humbled. Our own failures and shortcomings will be as clear to us as anyone else's. It will feel right to show mercy, for we receive mercy. Our isolating selfishness and vainglory fall away. We begin to have a sense of true equality, one that comes from seeing how we are all equally in need of God's grace. That grace knits our disparate lives together into family, friendship and community.

Rehearsals for Heaven.

What does the
Lord require
of you? but to do
JUSTICE
and to love
MERCY
and to walk
humbly with your
GOD.

Micah, chapter six,
verse eight

Fishing

Evangelism

I LIKE THIS QUOTE from John Buchan because it describes, with some wit, the avocation of fishing. On another level, it is an appealing way to think about evangelism — "Follow Me and I will make you fishers of men" (Mark 1:17). The Living Bible translates that as "fishermen for the souls of men." Perhaps I should look on my journeys from one arts and crafts show to another as "fishing trips."

Some souls seem elusive, yet by word and deed and in love we cast the nets of witness with steady faith. And it works, sometimes. On those occasions, it is the love — really — that makes it work. People may eventually prove susceptible, we may *catch* them, but only if they first sense that we genuinely love them. The opposite model of evangelism — "Become a Christian, join our club, and then we will accept you" — is, of course, not only offensive, but notoriously unsuccessful.

Fishermen don't insist on catching what is elusive, but they do have charming reasons for hope.

Bless the Lord

Adoration

I WAS DRIVING WEST on Route 58 early one morning, on my way from Virginia to North Carolina. It is a trip I often make. I pass croplands, small farms, little stands of pine, sycamore, oak. The road crosses a few creeks. The scenery is pleasant, though not what I would call breathtaking.

But on this one morning, on this singular journey, some window of my life, normally closed and shuttered, opened wide. I was overwhelmed. It was all, somehow, as beautiful to me, as astonishing and new, as the landscapes of Eden must have first seemed to Adam.

Edna St. Vincent Millay's poem "God's World" exults, "O world, I cannot hold thee close enough." I felt like that. I've driven Route 58 many times, before and since, same road, same scenery. That window opened only once, but I will never forget it.

The mnemonic ACTS reminds us of four kinds of prayer: adoration, contrition, thanks, supplication. It was adoration that was evoked so irresistibly that morning by the simple gifts of sky and woods and fields.

Psalm 103 proclaims adoration.

The charm of fishing + is that it is the pursuit of what is elusive, but attainable + a perpetual series of occasions for hope +

Bless the Lord,
O my soul, and all
that is within me,
bless his holy Name.
Psalm 103:1

Goethe

Communion

IT WAS MID-AFTERNOON of a busy day at one of the arts and crafts shows. I realized I hadn't eaten since breakfast. I said to the couple, who after some time had narrowed their choices to this Goethe and a quote from Saint Augustine, "I'm going to get some coffee and a sandwich. I'll be right back. May I bring you something?" "No thanks," they said. "You go ahead. We'll be right here trying to make up our minds."

When I returned they had selected the Goethe. We talked about the text. My ideas went something like this: "A particular poem, a certain picture, a favorite piece of music — these can become more than simple aesthetic experiences. What they can become is spiritual food. Just as we, at intervals, grow hungry for a meal — this snack of mine, for example — so God has designed us also to regularly grow hungry for Him. To regularly grow hungry for beauty. To satisfy this hunger, He nourishes us with Himself. He does this in many ways. The Creator feeds us beauty through art and nature. He reveals Himself to us in scripture. In the Lord's Supper He offers divine sustenance to meet human need. "This is My body, given for you," says Jesus as He breaks bread and shares it with His friends. "This cup is the New Testament in My blood which is shed for you" (Luke 22:19-20).

The thought I want to share, the one that Goethe's words suggest to me, is that there are times when even these "lesser feasts" – the poem, the aria, the watercolor – can also be a kind of communion. They awaken, and feed, our hunger for Beauty.

A person
should hear
a little
music, read
a little poetry and
see a fine
picture
every day in
order
that worldly cares
may not
obliterate the
sense of
the beautiful
which
God has implanted
in the human
soul.

GOETHE

Vine

Freedom

It is significant that the branches "abide in" and grow from the vine. In that connection or relationship they are fruitful. They live a good life. If the branches are not connected to the vine, ultimately they cannot be fruitful. A phrase I have used elsewhere seems pertinent: "The Lord has promised to make us free, not independent."

So, a question that comes to mind right away is, if "the branch and the vine" is the model for our binding and dependent relationship to the Lord, how do we think about freedom? Talking to Pharaoh, Aaron and Moses speak of freedom this way: "The Lord God of Israel says, 'Let My people go, so they can worship Me'" (Exodus 5). Freedom is necessary, but it is freedom with a particular purpose. It is freedom within our relationship to God. Freedom and faith and fruitful obedience are inextricable.

A little digression here. I see it is almost six p.m., and I am beginning to wonder what to fix for dinner. I must stop by the grocery store on my way home. Hmmm. How about orzo, roast chicken, baby spinach, olives, lemons, garlic, feta cheese. A plan begins to come together in my mind. I'm getting hungry. I'm thinking about food, about cooking, about flavors. So, what does this have to do with freedom?

Appetites and flavors are gifts from God, to be enjoyed. But they make a poor substitute god. I read about what happened to the Israelites after they got their apparent freedom, and I sometimes feel I run the danger of a kindred vulnerability.

We can live in subtle subjugation to our appetites. We can call ourselves free, but how free are we? Technically, I suppose, the Israelites were free as soon as they had crossed the Red Sea. But, in spite of being protected by one miracle after another, they were still afraid, and in their fear they were still enslaved. And in their cravings they were still enslaved.

They grumbled, "This repulsive manna. What wouldn't we give for a nice cucumber salad and carp broiled with leeks, and honeydew melon" (Numbers 11:5). You can take the Israelites out of slavery, but how do you take the slavery out of the Israelites?

God simply asks us, "What are your priorities?" He says, "Appetites are fine with Me — My gift to you, in fact. But I have to be your number one appetite, your most urgent desire, your first love. And in that love you will find obedience

In the Gospel of Saint John, ch. 15, v. 5 — Jesus says, I am the vine, and ye are the branches — they that abide in me & I in them, the same shall bring forth much fruit; apart from me . . ye can do nothing.

(difficult term; it seems to be at odds with your immature notions of freedom). And, in that obedience — contradictory as it sounds — you will find true freedom."

As Tim Keller, pastor of Redeemer Presbyterian Church in New York City, likes to say, "There is no freedom from God, there is only freedom in God."

Saint Augustine
His Initiative

I HAVE HEARD IT SAID that you can encompass the meaning of the entire Old and New Testament with the single statement, "Salvation is of the Lord" (Jonah 2:9).

What moves me about this piece — graphically one of my favorites — is that the response is mine, but the deed is His.

I can take initiative in many things. I can decide to learn Spanish, I can plant a garden, I can get lessons in ballroom dancing, or take up chess, or join a new Bible study group. To some extent, I can become learned and able in my chosen pursuits.

It's not that way with God, and here is the difference. In our relationship with God, the pursuit is His. It is He who has chosen us, not the other way around (John 15:16). He speaks first, awakening response.

Even before I thought of myself as a Christian, Francis Thompson's "The Hound of Heaven" held great appeal for me.

Crown

Retrospection

"THERE ARE SOME DEFEATS more triumphant than victories."

The quote is from Michel de Montaigne, the French essayist. By the visual setting within a Crown of Thorns, I have placed his words in the context of the Crucifixion. I find the irony of the word "defeats" particularly sobering. If I did not have the advantage of almost two thousand years of hindsight; if — say — I had shared Passover with Jesus and the disciples in the upper room (Luke 22), I doubt that I would have comprehended the full meaning of, "This is My body. This is My blood." But, as the immediate consequences of His plan began to dawn on me, I probably would have objected, "No, no, this sacrifice is a terrible idea. You're still young and healthy. Why, You're just getting started. Think of all the good You can still do."

At this point, He might have simply sighed, shaken His head, and given me that "you-still-don't-get-it, do-you" look. And, presumably, I would not have been alone in this. What was unfolding must have seemed so appalling, so frightening, and so cruel.

Yet, He was resolute. And this must have felt like deep winter in our hearts. He would have seen this and tried to reassure us, "Believe Me, spring is just around the corner." In John 16:22, we read "Now you have sorrow; but I will see you again and your hearts will rejoice."

Wheat

Food

Every summer I am astounded all over again by the prodigious generosity of the vegetable garden. Fewer seeds than I can grasp between my thumb and forefinger produce a multitude of salads … or more tomatoes than one family can possibly use.

What becomes of the individual seed on the way to accomplishing this increase? It goes into the earth and, as a seed, it disintegrates, it breaks apart. In a sense, it dies. And the food we eat, similarly, must be broken, the grains of wheat ground, the grapes crushed — so that we may be healthy and whole.

In this picture, I wanted the long rectangle with the single grain of wheat buried at the base of the design to suggest a tomb.

Ralph Waldo Emerson writes, "Go out into a garden and examine a seed; examine the same plant in the bud, and then in the fruit, and you must confess the whole process a miracle, a perpetual miracle."

Jesus uses this "perpetual miracle" as a symbol of His role in our lives. "Take, eat. This is My body, broken for you" (I Corinthians 11:24). He is the spiritual food that sustains our life. "When you eat and when you drink," He reminds us, "think of Me."

The Word is food. "When Your words came, I ate them; they were my joy and my heart's delight" (Jeremiah 15:16).

S · A · I · N · T

JOHN

CH · 12 V · 24

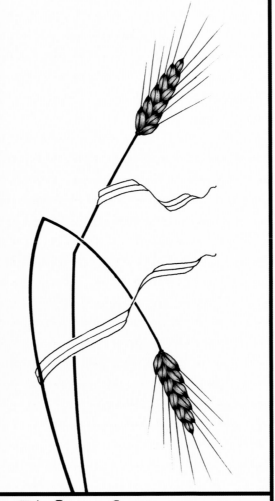

Truly, truly, I say to you ✠ except a grain of wheat falls into the earth and dies it remains alone ✠ but if it dies ✠ it bears much fruit.

Father

Born Again

WHEN SHOWING MY WORK in public, there was a question I used to get asked quite a bit. It struck me as straightforward, often to the point of bluntness, and generally came at the outset of the conversation. "Have you been born again?" I would usually pause a moment, wanting my answer to be not routine, but deliberate and suitably thoughtful.

"Well, yes," I would sometimes say, and let it go at that.

But at other times I wouldn't stop there. If as prominent a religious scholar as Nicodemus could puzzle over such a question for several lines in John's Gospel — with Jesus Himself right there offering enlightenment — then too quick or glib an assent on my part would not seem fitting. So, giving myself room to explore more extended meanings, I would say to my newfound acquaintance, "In fact, when my child was born, the man I had been until that very moment died, figuratively speaking, and was reborn." I don't think it is a bad answer. In a way, that birth had been a dual birth. Until that moment I had lived for myself primarily and — in all honesty — for others when I felt like it. Suddenly, everything had changed. This little person would not survive unless my wife and I cared for him and loved him.

"I will take away your heart of stone and give you a heart of flesh," we hear the Lord say in Ezekiel. God gives new birth. And in Matthew, Jesus tells us "I came not to be served, but to serve." That could be a practical definition of being born again. It is certainly one of the definitions of being a dad.

Behold I will
send you a prophet...
and he will turn
the hearts of the fathers
to the children
and the hearts of the children
to their fathers.
Malachi 4:5,6

fa•ther. -*vt.* To acknowledge responsibility for. Merriam-Webster

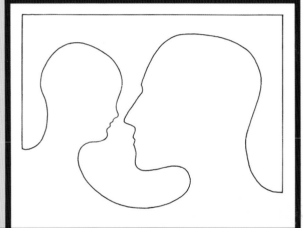

FATHER

I COULD NOT POINT TO ANY NEED IN
CHILDHOOD AS STRONG AS THAT FOR
A FATHER'S PROTECTION. S. FREUD

my earliest
model
for a
sense of God
was the
faith
wisdom and
open affection
of a loving
father

Mother

Adventure

YEARS AGO, I was doing an arts and crafts show in Philadelphia on Mother's Day weekend. Since I wasn't going to be with my mom to cook dinner or take her out, I wrote to her. The text on the right is an excerpt from my letter. As I wrote, I thought about our times together. I thought about growing up on an isolated ranch in Northern California, camping, swimming, raising cattle, chopping wood, riding horses. I thought about the move, a few years later, to Guadalajara, where she registered my sister and me in the local, rather than the English speaking, school. "You'll learn Spanish faster," our mom explained. (We did.) I remembered our travels, a few years later, around Ireland, and the home we lived in near Kinsale Harbour in County Cork. I remembered our two-year stay in Dublin. I remembered the great dinner parties she organized: actors, artists, writers, carpenters, house painters, musicians and students, all eating and drinking and talking for hours.

The characters and adventures from all the experiences we shared crowded together in my memory. I began to see the ways my life had grown out of her life. I realized that I had not grown up in a particular place. I had grown up in the vision and courage and faith of my mother.

HER
CHILDREN
RISE
UP AND
CALL
HER
BLESSED

CH 31 · V 28
PROV·

Mother

The place where I ✦
grew up was strong
and secure ✦ it was
bright and lovely·
It was my home ✦
it was the heart &
mind of my mother·

A PERSONAL REFLECTION

THY · CARE · HAS ·
PRESERVED · MY
SPIRIT · JOB X·XII

Children
Total Helplessness, Total Confidence

CONSIDER THESE THREE SENTENCES.

"Children are a heritage of the Lord" (Psalm 127:3).

"Except ye be converted and become as little children, ye shall not enter into the Kingdom of Heaven" (Matthew 18:3).

"Suffer the little children to come unto Me and forbid them not, for of such is the Kingdom of Heaven" (Luke 18:16).

What do these words from Psalms and the Gospels tell us about children? What quality is Jesus referring to when He says, "Except ye become as little children ...."? Certainly it is not carelessness or ignorance or self-centeredness. He is pointing toward something beautiful and desirable, something child-like, not childish.

I think of my own children, back to when they were simply children, in any of the nearly perpetual crises of their early lives — a bad dream, an injury at play, an illness — any fear or distress or pain. Their immediate need was expressed with one word, a cry "Mama!" or "Daddy!" There was no negotiation, no "Uh, Dad, when you have a minute, there's a little situation here we should perhaps discuss." No. It was total helplessness, total confidence.

This, Jesus is saying, is how you get into Heaven.

And it isn't only dire circumstances that prove instructive. I think of a three year old on an upper bunk: "Catch me, Daddy."

"No. It's time to go to sleep. We've had our stories. We've had our prayers. It's lights out, Pal."

"Oh, please. C'mon, just one time." He prevails. Exhilarated, eyes closed, he jumps — a perfection of trust. Being in a family teaches us so many things. That's what I'm trying to learn — or remember — now: how to fall into God.

While adulthood generally brings a sense of autonomy and self-reliance, the children in our lives are a reminder that we ourselves remain the children of God. In the dependency we see in these children, our own dependency is revealed.

CHILDREN

are a
heritage
of the
Lord.
psalm
127
verse
3

Gift of Peace

God gives us snow (Psalm 147:16).

I woke up to that peculiar stillness in the morning air and the upward cast of light through the bedroom window blinds. It had evidently snowed all night, five or six inches. Not enough to even mention to my friends in Maine, but this is southeastern Virginia and many secondary roads were impassable. No one came to work at our shop for two days.

Snow. Hardly the event that people with schedules, industrious people, welcome with much enthusiasm. Of course, the true enthusiasts, little children, just love it.

It was beautiful, exhilarating. The world outside was transformed. I made this "peace flakes" design soon afterwards because it seemed to me that transforming peace itself comes into our lives rather like the snow: quiet, gradual, initially unnoticed.

As our family worked its way through a long, lazy, snow-bound breakfast, I found myself thinking: *Actually, this is good. This is just what we needed.* The snow was a timely cure for some vague condition that had been creeping up on us. The symptoms had been a sense of tedium and weariness with the routines of work and school, an absence — I realized — of just this: pure delight, spontaneous, unbidden.

I know it's not just snow at work here. It's God (again). He's versatile, knows our needs, enjoys surprises.

.. a gift of peace, quietly descending, blankets the terrain of the heart

Psalm 139

The Companion

AMID THE VAST AND TOWERING IMAGERY in this Psalm, what is particularly appealing to me is the simple assurance of the Lord's abiding presence in my life. He is intimate, personal, no matter where I am, no matter where I go. I need to let that sink in.

My petitionary prayers are inconsistent, random. They wander. The subjects are my family, friends, myself, people I hear about... the usual. "Please do this. Please do this."

I can imagine the Lord saying, "I'm glad you're praying, Michael, turning to Me with these various needs. Of course, that's the right thing to do. But has it ever occurred to you that sometimes you could just keep Me company? Do you ever want to — as your son likes to say — 'just hang out'?"

"Speaking of needs," He continues, "Your deepest need is not to have Me change this or that situation in your life. Your deepest need *is* to have Me in your life. Do you see the difference?"

L·O·R·D

✤ whither shall I go
from thy spirit? or
whither shall I flee
from thy presence?
if I ascend up in—
to heaven ✤ behold
Thou art there. If
I make my bed in
hell ✤ behold Thou
art there. If I take
the wings of the
morning and dwell
in the uttermost
parts of the sea ✤
even there shall thy
hand lead me and
thy right hand ✤✤
shall hold me

PSALM 139:7-10

Ask
Need

ON A WINTER NIGHT many years ago, I was returning from an arts and crafts show in Ohio. It was very cold. The heater in the van wasn't working, but the cassette player was. I listened to Jessye Norman singing Richard Strauss. Glorious as the music was — *The Four Last Songs*, as I recall — I eventually grew too weary to drive. I pulled into a rest stop and, bundling up in a watch cap and an old pea jacket I kept in the van, I slept. But not for long; the cold woke me up. I got back on the road. Jessye sang for me again. The warmth of her voice contrasted, not only with the cold, but with a strange sense of desolation I had begun to feel — the result, I suppose, of still being so far from home, my exhaustion, and — odd as it sounds — the depressingly scruffy state of the pea jacket ("I've got to get this thing to the cleaners," I told myself).

I probably made seventy-five miles before my head began to nod again. I pulled into another rest stop, reluctantly turning off the music, my bulwark against the cold night. This time I dreamt. It was cold in the dream, too. I was on a dark, narrow cobblestone street. Each door I passed was closed, each window shuttered. Then I came to a brightly lit window. I looked in. There was a long table set for a meal with candles and crystal and fine linen. A fireplace blazed nearby. Graceful men and women, all dressed in long white garments, conversed in groups and moved about the room. One of the men saw me at the window. He came, opened the door, and with a voice of surpassing kindness, invited me in. I felt totally abashed. "No, I couldn't," I said. Somehow, I was still wearing the wretched pea jacket. "You people are clean and fine and beautiful, and look at me. I'm a mess. I'm dirty and tired. I've been on the road." "It's all right," the man reassured me. "We have clothing for you. You can bathe, then you can rest if you feel like it. Actually, we've been waiting for you."

Sometimes when we're knocking, we don't even know it. But God does, and He is generous and faithful.

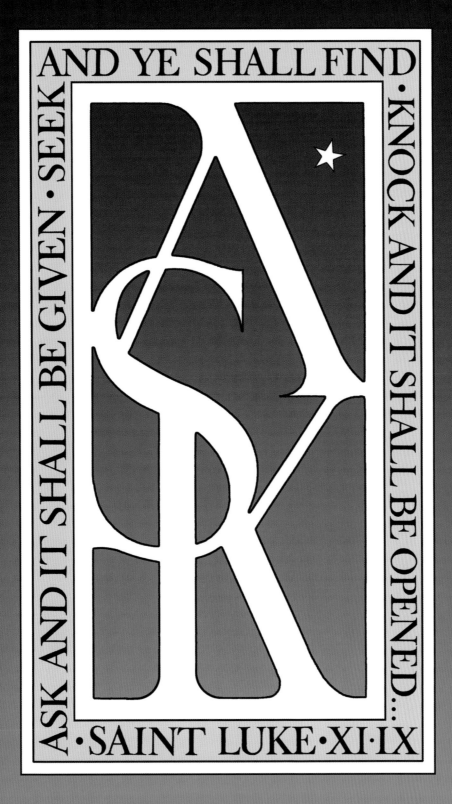

ASK AND IT SHALL BE GIVEN • SEEK AND YE SHALL FIND • KNOCK AND IT SHALL BE OPENED... • SAINT LUKE • XI • IX

Thou

Gratitude

THIS TEXT COMES TO US from the 17th century English poet George Herbert. The idea does seem somewhat circular — "I shall be grateful for the gift of ... gratitude?" — but the paradox reveals something profound.

When I try to imagine life without a sensed relationship to God — troubled and perplexing though that relationship sometimes feels — what I find myself missing, among other things, is simply someone to thank.

How do we respond to a true gift? The incomparable excellence of yet another morning. The face, the touch of a loved one. A new insight. Favorite music. Faith that awakens us to God's promise. Recovery from a serious illness or accident. A surprising act of kindness. The obvious, almost unthinking response to these is some expression of gratitude, "Thank you, Lord." When a crisis passes, even the nonbeliever may come up with a spontaneous "O, thank God," followed, perhaps, by an inward "Oops. Where did that come from?"

Simply put, since there are gifts, the believer assumes there must be a Giver. The *You* in "thank you."

Thou

HAST GIVEN
SO MUCH · TO
US · GIVE ONE
THING MORE
· A GRATEFUL
HEART ·

Hear, O Israel

One God

THERE ARE DESCRIPTIONS in Exodus of embroideries and draperies in the Tabernacle, of priestly robes, of dyes and gems and gold. The color scheme is consistent: crimson and purple and blue. Later, in II Chronicles, when Solomon is directing the construction of the Temple, he makes decorative use of these same colors. These historical details are the basis for this design.

I had been planning to take my work to a large religious convention where, unsurprisingly, some major controversies were anticipated. This text had been on my mind for some time. I felt that its message of fundamental unity of belief might be welcomed as a reminder of common ground. So, with my extensive display of pictures in place (Old Testament, New Testament, a little philosophy, a little poetry), I was caught somewhat off guard on hearing "Well, well. Something for everyone." Then my ironic visitor stopped at the Deuteronomy 6:4, "even the monotheists."

I still think it may have helped a bit.

שמע
HEAR

ישראל
O ISRAEL

יהוה אלהינו
THE LORD OUR GOD

יהוה אחד
THE LORD IS ONE

Rich

Us

"R-i-c-h. The 'h' is lower case," I explain, because at first people seem to have difficulty finding it.

My friend, the late Jack I. Kohler is the author. After he shared it with me, I said "Jack, I'd like to letter that. I would work your initials into the design as a credit."

Occasionally I am asked, "Now, does 'who you have beside you' refer to a friend or a spouse? Or is it the Lord?" "It's all of them," I usually say.

I'm thinking of God in Genesis concluding each stage of Creation and pronouncing it "good," over and over. But, what is the first "not good"? Of course it is when God determines that it is "not good for the man to be alone." And this despite the fact Adam was already experiencing a relationship with his Creator.

The idea of marriage, family, friendship and community seems to be at the heart of God's plan for us. Most often, we get to know Him beside one another and looking together in His direction.

IS NOT HOW MUCH
YOU HAVE ~ ~ OR
WHERE YOU ARE
GOING ~ OR EVEN
WHAT YOU ARE ~
RICH IS WHO YOU
HAVE BESIDE YOU
~ ~ JIK·II

Love Never Fails
The Mainstay

INTELLECT FAILS.
Looks fail.
Skills fail.
Cultures fail.
Careers fail.
Batteries fail.
Investments fail.
Eyesight fails.
Charm fails.
Health fails.
Recipes fail.
Kings fail.
Religious leaders fail.
An artist fails.
Love never fails.
When it looked like love had failed, on closer exami-
nation, we always discovered it was really something
else.

LOVE

Saint Paul's first letter

NEVER

to the Corinthians, chapter

FAILS

thirteen, verse eight ✤ NIV

Two Stars
Generosity

THIS PIECE WAS A REQUEST from a Jewish family in Virginia Beach. It was for their daughter's marriage, and comes from a rabbi known as the Baal Shem Tov, which means Master of the Good Name.

I recall having some difficulty with the design. The usual left to right, top to bottom didn't seem to work. What I was trying to achieve was a movement of the words that would reflect the upward direction of the text — "From every human being there rises a light…." The family was very patient with me, and when the picture was finally done — alas, some while after the wedding — they seemed grateful and genuinely pleased.

What appealed to me in the message was the way it challenged me to think about my relationship to God — "a light that reaches straight to heaven." I thought about becoming that "single brighter light" in my relationships of marriage and family. But how do we do that? How are we transformed into that single brighter light? These relationships inevitably demand that I give, that I serve. This is not always agreeable. Sometimes it leads to conflict. When I am called on to share my time, my resources, there seems to be markedly less for me. God, however, takes a different view of the matter. He says, "All life, all your resources, time and love itself, all come from Me anyway. Your wife, your children, your neighbors: their needs are your needs. Be generous. Share Me."

So, that single brighter light is the love, the generosity I am being encouraged to express.

During the idyllic stage, the early stage, in Eden, I can imagine Adam's astonishment to find that the love he felt for God — far from being diminished by being shared with Eve — had in fact increased and grown even brighter.

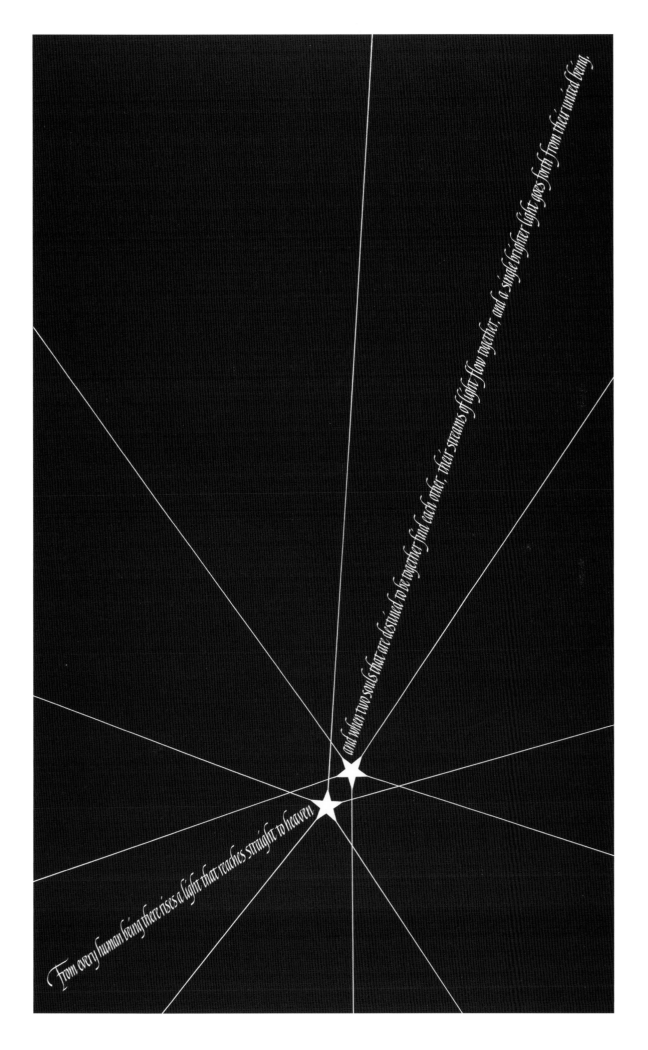

From every human being there rises a light that reaches straight to heaven

and when two souls that are destined to be together find each other, their streams of light flow together, and a single brighter light goes forth from their united being

Sing

The Joyful Noise

WHY ARE SINGING AND JOY AND PRAISE so closely connected? I can't say. But I have experienced an irresistible gladness on hearing the music at Sunday Service.

Once, on a special occasion some years ago, we had the "Laudate Dominum" from Mozart's *Solemn Vespers*. Now, whenever I think of how the music struck me that day I am, curiously, reminded of a small child who is given a helium balloon — it usually seems to be red. He is told, "Now, hold onto this tight." And he does, briefly. But then, overcome by wonder and delight, he forgets, his fist unclenches, and his cherished balloon floats away, up to Heaven. (He usually gets another one.)

Whenever I hear Kiri Te Kanawa, or almost any other soprano, sing those opening notes of Mozart's "joyful noise," something in me does the same thing — floats away, in helpless delight and praise, up to Heaven.

SING

Make a joyful noise unto the Lord·
serve the Lord with gladness· come before his presence
with singing·

Book of Psalms · chapter one
hundred · verses one & two

Symphony
Fortune

FROM MY FIRST LOOK through our kitchen window while fixing the morning coffee, until my last at dusk amid preparations for supper, I am continually and abundantly rewarded by what I see. It is a fairly common view revealing a small creek — a tributary of the James River — which is subject to the tides of the Chesapeake Bay. So, through the pines, laurels, gums, and oaks, whether in rain or snow or sunshine, I see marshland or water, or some regularly varying combination of both.

From day to day and season to season, the view, of course, comprises other changing elements, creates odd varying impressions. A scattering of dogwood petals one afternoon in late spring is like a fleeting memory of snow in January. A couple of months later, I glimpse one red leaf on the gum tree. "But that's too soon," something in me protests, "it's just July... I'm still young."

And there are creatures: heron, songbirds, squirrel, muskrat, an occasional tortoise or black snake. I have found signs of raccoons, but they work the nightshift, and I seldom see them.

I have never gotten around to doing much cultivation of the property. It is hardly a monument to my achievement. Yet, by means that are both "unbidden and unconscious," it ministers to me deeply.

*To be content
with small means · to seek
elegance rather than luxury · and refinement
rather than fashion · to be worthy
· not respectable · and wealthy · not rich ·
to study hard · think quietly · talk gently · act frankly ·
to listen to stars and birds · to babes and sages with open heart
· to bear all cheerfully · do all bravely ·
await occasions · hurry never ·
In a word · to let the spiritual · unbidden and
unconscious · grow up through
the common · this is to be
my symphony ·*

W · H · C H A N N I N G

One of our sons lives here with us. He is a constant reader, a writer, a wood-worker, a thoughtful fellow. Whenever there has been some unexpected hiatus in his routine of work or school, resulting in days or weeks of unstructured time, I have never given him much specific advice. He's bright, he'll figure it out. But I have offered the suggestion that in the midst of deciding "what next," he should not neglect to grasp the simple gift of this time and this place: the heron in the creek patiently stalking her breakfast, the afternoon deep gold of the marsh grass, the faint sweet scent of the Russian olive hedge.

These are not themselves the gift, they are just the wrapping. The gift is peace, a sense of perfect completeness, Shalom.

He listens. I go on, "What if you were to move someplace else? And you might. Someplace where there are no trees? No tall, uncritical pines, no frolicking laurels? What if you lived in an apartment and your only view was of other apartments? Your sense of this land, this creek, this moment, might turn out to be like a wise investment you had made, like wealth, something you could live on."

Do Good

Service

AFTER HURRICANE FLOYD in 1999, our son Joshua came home to discover our entire downstairs flooded, six inches more or less. He did the right thing. He called our neighbor Jim, who, as it happens, runs a carpet cleaning business. It's exactly what I would have done, had I been at home. Jim stepped through the door, took one look around, and went into action. He drove to his shop, returned with his cleaning van, and removed hundreds of gallons of water from the floor of our house. He pitched in with all the work that followed: moving furniture, drying the carpet, replacing padding.

Jim's initial reaction, the one that guided all his succeeding efforts, was the simple question, "How can I help?" There are experiences in which God, unmistakably, makes Himself known to us through our friends.

In my two sons' activities and accomplishments in school and in the workplace, I am beginning to see the outlines of careers. I have never offered them much particular counseling in this connection, other than to express the hope that, on encountering the chaos, want, and pain of this life, they would roll up their sleeves and say, "How can I help?"

DO

all the good you can ❖ ❖
by all the means you can
❖ in all the ways you can,
in all the places you can ❖
❖ at all the times you can,
to all the people you can ❖
❖ as long as ever you can

JOHN WESLEY

I Can Do

Plans

THOUGH WELL ATTENDED, the craft show for me had been a very slow one. Another exhibitor asked, "How's it going?" I commented ruefully that my calligraphy might as well be in Sanskrit, for all the interest it had attracted.

I could read Paul's words to the Philippians from where I sat (and sat, and sat): "I have learned to be content in all circumstances. I know what it is to be hungry and what it is to be full. I know what it is to be in need." Then he concludes, triumphantly, "I can do all things through Christ Who strengthens me." If Paul could do all things, I wondered, why was he hungry? Why was he in need?

What he means, I think, is that he can do all things within the context of Christ's will, Christ's plan for him. If the plan involves a banquet, OK. If a week later there's nothing to eat, OK. Contented, he moves through scarcity and abundance. A human plan, a practical plan would at least have focused on the resources to assure Paul three meals a day and adequate lodging. It might even have regularly set a little something aside for retirement. But Paul is not like the arrogant hero of Henley's "Invictus"; he is not the *master of his fate*. When Paul says, so confidently, that he "can do all things … ," he doesn't even know what those things might be. Who could plan such a life?

I continued to sit in my chair. The show began to take on a different perspective.

Paul's faith beckons.

I have learned to be content in all circumstances.

I know what it is to be in need and what it is to have plenty. I know what it is to be hungry and what it is to be full. I can do all things through Christ who strengthens me.

Phil. four : eleven to thirteen

I Am

Who is Jesus?

WHAT COLOSSAL CLAIMS. Others have pointed out the way, have given us guidelines and examples. But this man is totally different. Instead of "This is the path to perfection," He says, "I am Perfection, and I am also the Path to Perfection." The premise is that Truth, which had always been objective, became — shockingly, scandalously — an actual human being.

So, what are we to make of these I AM statements? They are so direct, so absolute. They force us to choose, just like when Jesus says flat out, "The Father and I are One" (John 10:30). Such an assertion cannot be dismissed or avoided or watered down. How do we respond? Do we say, "You may be a great teacher, a spiritual master. But 'one with God'? Isn't that a bit much?" Or do we recognize His claims as unequivocal, allowing no neutral middle ground. He must be everything He claims to be — or else a lunatic and a liar.

In Matthew 16:15 Jesus asks Peter, "Who do you say that I am?" "You are Christ, the Son of the Living God," Peter responds. "Right," says Jesus, "and you didn't figure that out on your own, either. My Father in Heaven revealed it to you."

As we earnestly confront that same question — Who is Jesus? — I like to think that the answer could, just possibly, come to us as readily and as unmistakably as it did to Peter.

I AM

the bright and morning star ✦
the resurrection and the life
✦ the true vine ✦ the light of
the world ✦ the bread of life
✦ the good shepherd ✦ the way,
the truth, and the life ✦ the
gate ✦ Alpha and Omega, the
first and the last ✦✦

ST. JOHN · REVELATION

II Chronicles

Salvation

FOR A FEW MONTHS in my early twenties I worked for a diving company. I was a crew member on a small work boat in the San Francisco Bay. We had completed repairs on the propeller of a freighter. The water was choppy, and we were looking at more than two hours for the trip back to our home pier. Maintenance chores were ongoing, and the oil in one of the compressors had been changed earlier in the day. A crew member passed me a five gallon bucket filled with the spent oil. "Take this up on deck and throw it overboard when you get a chance. Watch your step." "I can't do that," I said. My companion replied, "Why not? It will just go away." Instead, I took the oil back to the pier and dropped it off at a filling station on my way home that evening.

His words "It will just go away" stuck in my mind. One doesn't have to be a marine biologist to see the problem.

We have grown chary of using the word *sin* in everyday circumstances, yet it seems to me the word that best describes the prospect of a sheet of filthy oil, even a relatively small sheet of filthy oil, floating out into one of God's great oceans. And, like the oil, sin never "just goes away."

I was pondering how this image applies to my own life. I had in mind all those "bad steward" incidents when I had failed to "take the oil back to the filling station." I remembered base thoughts, hurtful words, and wretched deeds. The recollection, of course, makes me feel terrible. The word *sin* is sometimes inescapable, and so is the word *guilt*.

There was always that first appalling realization, "Now look at what I have done, and there is nothing I can do to change it. I can't take back the words. I can't hit *delete*." Explanations and apologies might have followed. Shame and remorse might have changed subsequent behavior. I do hope so. The heart yearns for atonement. But wrong, the sin itself, stubbornly won't go away. Like the dirty oil, where would it go? Accountability remains. And this accountability creates a great impasse.

This verse from the Old Testament mentions sin and the forgiveness of sin, and my thoughts jump ahead to the New. Here, once more, I ask the familiar questions: What does Christ's life mean to me personally? Why did He come? And, inevitably, Why did He have to die?

I see Jesus stepping into the middle of that impasse my sin has caused. He

If My people

who are called by my name, shall humble themselves ✤ and pray and seek my face ✤ and turn from their ✤ wicked ways; then I will hear from heaven ✤ and will forgive their sin ✤ and will heal their land ✤

2 CHRONICLES
7:14

---

says, "You were made to be loving and compassionate, to be openhearted. But over and over you have closed your heart, you have turned away. This is sin, and it has to be accounted for. Justice demands it."

Then, fully aware of the hell He is about to undergo — humiliation, inconceivable pain, utter alienation — He says, "Here is what I will do. O My Father, Judge of all, accept My innocent and substitutionary death as an atonement for all Michael's sin. Forgive his wrongs, past, present, and — You know how he is — future as well. I am wealthy in goodness and love and Michael is destitute. Accept My sacrifice as payment of his debt." Why would Jesus do this? He answers, "My brother has become bankrupt, and as such, a captive. No one else has the wealth or power or goodness to bail him out. But that doesn't completely answer the *Why* question, does it? The fact is, I love him and therefore I want him to be free."

Be Strong

Security

I HAD BEEN MEANING to letter this Deuteronomy text for some time and finally finished it in early September a few years ago. I was at an arts and crafts show on the thirteenth of that month in 2001.

I noticed a young man studying my display intently. It was this text that he was reading over and over. Finally, he turned to me. "I had to get out of the house. I've been pretty much glued to the TV for the last couple of days. I needed to hear something else. I guess this was what I needed."

Last fall a friend of mine, who is a physician, said, "If you haven't had your flu shot yet, come on by the office and I'll fix you up." I got the shot. I believe it helped. I take vitamin C and some other supplements. My diet is basically wholesome. Years ago, at the urging of friends and relatives, I stopped swimming in the ocean during thunderstorms. (My excuse had been that if the fish were all right, I would be too.) I have some health and life insurance.

I'm not against precaution. Environmental laws, traffic regulations, national security, and a whole host of other protections have a sound basis. They make sense. Still, I must add that I doubt I was in any real peril back when I drank hot coffee from cups that failed to warn me in three languages that the coffee was hot. At times it seems to me we are striving for an existence in which every mortal and lesser danger is under our control, every risk perfectly calculated. And yet, fears and anxieties abide. Troubles persist.

My point — admittedly a paradoxical one — is that while all our varied defenses and safeguards are useful, they offer only an attempt at security, never a guarantee. True security is what the Lord promises when He says, "I will not leave you or forsake you."

62

BE
STRONG
and of good courage ✦
Do not fear, for the Lord your God
✦ *goes with you.*
He will not leave you
or forsake you ✦
DEUTERONOMY
31:6

Pruning Hooks

Peace

IT'S BEEN LIKE THIS FOR YEARS. I don't read the newspapers or watch TV that much. But, if I'm driving to an art show or working in my office, I will often turn on the radio. That's when I get the news. And it never really seems to change. I guess I'm about ninety-eight percent numb to it by now: "wars and rumors of war," violence, hatred, bloody reprisals. From time to time, though, something connects. The terrible hurt in the report I've just heard hits home, cutting through my apathy. "O, Lord," I find myself saying, though it's really more of a groan, "is all this cruelty ever going to end?" A fairly common reaction, I imagine.

"Yes. As a matter of fact, it is going to end," He promises us in the second chapter of Isaiah. And I find it a comfort to think about that as I reread these verses.

I was recently trying to share my ideas about this with a friend. "What?" he said right off the bat. "You think the invasion was a mistake?" "Maybe it was, maybe it wasn't. We don't know yet," I said. "That's not my point here. This is about the future. What this scripture is telling us is that one day, hard as it is to believe, there really will be peace, there really will be disarmament: you know, 'pruning hooks,' 'plowshares.' And, obviously, not just us, the other guys as well. Imagine a small group of terrorists assembling an explosive device to blow up ... what? The UN Headquarters? the residence of the ambassador from Timbuktu? One of them has an epiphany. He puts down his screwdriver and the wire he was attaching to the detonator. 'Hey. Wait a minute guys,' he says. 'I just had an idea. Listen. What do you say, instead of a car bomb, we use this vehicle for Meals on Wheels?' He makes a gesture like a scales, arms stretched out, palms open, raising and lowering them. 'Think about it,' he says, nodding to his left, 'car bomb?', then to his right, 'Meals on Wheels?'"

ISAIAH 2:4

He shall judge
among the nations ✢
and settle disputes for
many peoples, and
they ✢ shall beat their
swords into plowshares
and their spears into
pruning hooks ✢
nation shall not lift up
sword against nation,
neither shall they
learn war anymore ✢

Armor of Light
The Breadth of Grace

How ARE WE TO REACT to the incidents of violence and cruelty that confront us regularly? The darkness we experience? The darkness we simply hear about? The darkness we perpetrate by unkindness, however slight?

As a design, I wanted the "light" to be greater than the dark area it surrounds, and I wanted to pierce holes in the darkness.

Showing sympathy toward those who are hurt feels right. Praying for them feels right. But, praying for the criminal, the maniac, the tyrant — that's hard to do. It often just feels impossible. One of the obstacles I encounter is my first reaction, which usually is "That's outrageous, unthinkable" — and it is — followed by an implicit "I'd never do anything like that."

My prayers, if I'm praying at all, often assume a clear moral separation. I am on one side; the "bad guys" are on the other.

Miroslav Volf says, "Forgiveness breaks down when we exclude the wrongdoer from the community of humans, and ourselves from the community of sinners."

Of course, I insist on justice. But, if I don't also insist on mercy, where does that leave me? Am I not also in daily need of mercy?

When I ask for the grace to cast away the works of darkness, I know that while another's "works of darkness" may be more lurid and shocking than mine, we are both destructive. Our need to be covered by the Armor of Light is the same. My prayers need to encompass both victim and victimizer, for I am both.

Now, in the time of this mortal life, Almighty God, give us grace to cast away the works of darkness, and put on the armor of light.

Enthusiasm

Word Roots

I COPIED THIS DEFINITION out of the dictionary.
It's enough to make one enthusiastic about etymology.

Follow Me

Eternal Comfort

A CHARMING, LIVELY, WHITE-HAIRED LADY named Ruth came into my gallery recently. She noticed the "Follow Me" and said, "I'm just going to have to buy that one. It's my verse, you know." "Why is that?" I asked.

"When I was ten years old I had a very vivid dream," she explained. "Our Lord was standing before me, looking right into my eyes. He held my gaze for some time. But at the point where I was sure He was going to tell me something, He just turned and walked away. When I awoke I remembered the dream — of course — and it depressed me. In fact, for the next several years the memory of it — of Him turning His back on me — always made me kind of sad. Years later, when I was a young woman, about twenty, going to college, the Lord again appeared to me in a dream, basically the same dream. Again He was looking directly at me. But this time He spoke, 'Ruth, when I turned and walked away, it was because I expected you to follow Me.' After that, whenever I remembered the first dream, of course, it didn't bother me anymore. In fact, it made me glad. And all those recurrent memories of the first dream during my teens — they no longer made me sad, in fact they became a source of joy."

Now, whenever I look at "Follow Me," I think of Ruth. I think of the Lord healing our whole existence, redeeming even the past. I think of being absolved of all the fears, antagonisms, failures, wraths, and sorrows, actual and remembered, which we carry around with us. I think of exchanging all that for His "light burden and easy yoke" (Matthew 11:30).

en·thū´si·asm(!)*n.*[<Greek:*enthousiasmos,*< *en,*in+*theos,*God] 1. An exalted or ecstatic feeling. en-thu´si-as´tic, *adj.* To be inspired by God, to be possessed by God.

"FOLLOW ME" *He said.*

Matthew 4:19

Bread

Perception

A FEW YEARS AGO, in the early spring, my sister, who works in the health care field, told me, "You better come soon if you want a good visit with Mom." She used words like "untreatable" and "weeks not months." That is why I was in California that Easter.

Sara had warned me, "Don't be shocked when you see her. She's lost a lot of weight. And it's not like she had it to spare." An odd detail still sticks in my mind. Her earlobes were like little paper flower petals and showed no evidence of flesh. Far stronger than this impression, though, is my memory of how, within ten minutes, I became quite unaware of the way the illness had altered her appearance. The reason, of course, was simply the deep pleasure we felt in being together. The subject that often comes to my mind at this point is the influence of God's Spirit on our perceptions.

In the Gospel of John, Mary Magdalen is weeping at the empty tomb. "Where is He?" she implores a man she believes to be the gardener. Actually, the man is Jesus, but she doesn't recognize Him. Then He speaks her name, "Mary." She knows Him at once and is filled with joy.

In the Gospel of Luke, Jesus joins two of his followers a little way outside Jerusalem on the road to Emmaus. Like Mary, they are not aware of who He is. "You seem deeply troubled. What's the matter?" He asks them. They reply, "What's the matter?! You mean you haven't heard?" And they tell Him about their crisis, the arrest and execution of the One they had believed was the Redeemer of Israel, the Savior. Then, addressing their feelings of abandonment and despair, Jesus gently reminds them of all the prophecies about the Messiah as revealed through Moses and the Prophets, how every promise had been fulfilled. "The plan for salvation is right on course," He assures them. (Of course, He is talking about Himself.)

Evening comes, they stop at an inn for supper. They have spent most of the day together, yet it is only at the table, when He breaks the bread, that they suddenly recognize who He is. (Perhaps they were reminded of another breaking of the bread a few nights earlier.)

They came to know him in the BREAK-ing of the BREAD. LUKE 24:35

Finally, I want to refer to another story, one that is very familiar and very dear to many of us. It expresses an underlying truth that, I think, connects each of the above accounts: the visit with my mom as well as the two Gospel narratives.

In *The Little Prince*, Saint-Exupéry writes of the farewell between the prince and his friend the fox. "Goodbye," says the fox, "And now here is my secret, a very simple secret: it is only with the heart that one can see rightly; what is essential is invisible to the eye."

Imagine
Immortality

THE MAN AND HIS WIFE stopped at my exhibit. They must have been in their late seventies or early eighties. He was walking very slowly, breathing oxygen from a tank mounted on a small trolley he pushed. She was sturdier and followed him closely. He was frail, but peaceful. She seemed to have the weight of the world on her shoulders. He read the "Imagine."

"Those words sure take on more meaning when you're getting close to the end," he said calmly, almost cheerfully. I was moved, but for the moment, couldn't think of a reply. The line from the picture, "Imagine breathing new air...," ran through my mind. The expression on his wife's face remained unchanged. He started to leave, but hesitated. "That reminds me. I had a dream. Oh, it must have been about two weeks ago. I'm in the den at our house." Here he nodded toward his wife. "The den is fairly dark, but it opens onto the kitchen, which has plenty of light, especially in the morning, since we have a big picture window that faces east. But, I don't remember it ever being that bright. Well, in the dream, all that happens is that I'm walking out of the dark den into the bright light of the kitchen. Then I hear this voice." His wife turned, watching him more intently. "I know this is going to sound weird," he said, "but I knew it was God's voice, and all He said was, 'It's as simple as that, Frank.'"

IMAGINE

stepping onto a shore and finding it heaven

IMAGINE

taking hold of a hand and finding it God's hand

IMAGINE

breathing new air and finding it celestial air

IMAGINE

feeling invigorated and finding it immortality

IMAGINE

passing from storm & tempest to an unknown calm

IMAGINE

waking and finding it home—

Candle

Pity the Afflicted

MY DAUGHTER AT SEVENTEEN was six feet two inches tall, had green eyes, blond wavy hair, and was considered by almost everyone to be alarmingly beautiful.

I don't know if there is any use in trying to separate and define the different kinds of suffering. But, when she died in a traffic accident in 1994, it seems to me my most bitter realization was that I would never see her again.

As an artist, I have a keen visual attachment to the physical world, to my friends, to my family. The thought that her face was forever gone from my sight was terrible. It was the thought with which I woke in the morning and the one with which I went to sleep at night. Then, one night about three weeks after the accident — three abjectly miserable weeks — I had a dream. I was at an arts and crafts show, one where she had helped me on a couple of occasions. I was sitting at a picnic table on the grounds. It was a fine sunny day. She walked up and sat down across from me. "Kezziah," I said, "I am so glad to see you. I know you're just here for a visit and can't stay long (somehow I understood that), but this is so great! I'll tell you how glad I am to see you. While you're here, I'm not even going to let myself blink." (And I remember in the dream how my eyes fixed on her face with rapt attention, refusing the reflex to close for so much as a fraction of a second.) Our conversation was happy, lighthearted. After a little while she left. When I woke up, I sensed that a change, a transformation was underway. The chaotic, all encompassing pain had begun to subside. Of course, I still missed her terribly, and continue to, but that devestating I'll-never-see-her-again ache was gone.

My guess as to what prompted the dream? I imagine she said something like, "Lord, my dad is so bummed out about me being gone. Just look at him. Can't we do something for him?" "Yes, you're right, Kezziah," God says. "I'll tell you what. Tonight, when he goes to sleep, I'll fix it up so that you just go and have a little visit with him. That should do the trick."

"And God shall wipe away all the tears from their eyes…." Revelation 21:4

1.

Keep watch · Dear Lord ·
with those who work ·
or watch ✤ or weep this
night · and give your
angels charge over ✤
those who sleep ✤
Tend the sick ✤ Lord

2.

Christ · give rest to the
weary ✤ bless the dying ·
soothe the suffering ✤
pity the afflicted ✤
shield the joyous · and
all for your love's ✤✤✤
sake · Amen THE BOOK OF
COMMON PRAYER

Desert

Bethlehem

The word *bedlam* has an interesting background. The priory originally known as Saint Mary of Bethlehem, constructed around 1245 in London, was, by the late Middle Ages, being used as a lunatic asylum. *Bedlam* is derived from *Bethlehem.*

The September through mid-December stretch on the arts and crafts show circuit can feel like a very long trek. I am almost always away from home. I arrive in Atlanta...Baltimore...Charlotte...Philadelphia...locate the show site; figure out where to register; wait in line; get my booth number; set up the exhibit; look for lodging.

As the days grow shorter and the weather colder, all this transient activity takes on a hectic quality: lots of driving, obviously; talking at length to groups of people, to individuals; long weary hours; catch-as-catch-can meals; and, of course, setup and breakdown, with their special uproars and confusions.

In some city, during my pre-Christmas travels, a few years ago, the idea occurred to me, *I know where I am. I have come into Bethlehem. And, as it happens, it's not the census, it's my work that brings me here. Right now, this work is what I do, and, really, am glad to do. Right now, the circumstances probably cannot be changed. Actually, the circumstances are temporary, and they are OK. But I can change. I can see things in a different way. I can see people in a different way. I can receive grace here. Through all the busyness and hubbub, I can still hear that knock at the door, and welcome Him when He appears, in whatever guise, and say, "Come in, come in. Of course there's room for You."*

I have never been able to locate a definite source for this text. It was sent to me years ago on a Christmas card with no attribution.

IF · AS HEROD · WE FILL OUR LIVES WITH THINGS · AND AGAIN WITH THINGS · IF WE
CONSIDER OURSELVES SO UNIMPORTANT THAT WE MUST FILL EVERY MOMENT
OF OUR LIVES WITH ACTION · WHEN WILL WE HAVE TIME TO MAKE THE LONG SLOW
JOURNEY ACROSS THE DESERT AS DID THE MAGI? OR SIT AND WATCH THE STARS
AS DID THE SHEPHERDS? OR BROOD OVER THE COMING OF THE CHILD AS DID MARY?
FOR EACH ONE OF US THERE IS A DESERT TO TRAVEL · A STAR TO DISCOVER · AND A
BEING WITHIN OURSELVES TO BRING TO LIFE

Holy Christmas & Shepherds

Renewal

WE WERE ENGULFED in the massive upheaval of moving house. Crates, boxes, packing material everywhere. I placed a large shallow ceramic bowl on a card table, preparing to envelop it in bubble wrap. It had been a gift to me, sent from Japan. A brushed design in the blue-green glaze depicted two carp. With the bowl half full of water, and — depending on the season — with a few azalea blossoms or some red Bradford pear leaves floating on the surface, the effect was of a quiet woodland stream or pool. So natural were the two images in the glaze, that at the first surprised glimpse, one felt moved to say, "Oh, I just saw a fish!"

I suppose that the children were reminded not to run while indoors as often in our house as any other. Nevertheless, my four-year-old son Joshua was running through the cluttered living room. He caught his foot on the leg of the card table, and my bowl fell to the floor, and it broke. I was very, very angry.

The move was completed. Joshua and I managed to overcome the matter of the broken bowl. But some tiny stubborn ache remained, a subconscious sense of damage, loss, a wound.

Many years later, after many Christmases in the new house, my wife and I decided that it would be fun, and certainly something different, to celebrate the holiday away from home. Our family took a winter cruise.

"Fun," as we all eventually learn, is an elusive condition, obtained, more often than not, inadvertently. However, in the matter of accomplishing something *different*, or even *odd*, we were brilliantly successful. The oddest time of all was Christmas Eve, as we floated around somewhere in the misty, incongruous Caribbean.

I felt moved to say something to the family about our Lord's birth and its promise, not a seasonal prayer or sermon; just a timely word or two to encourage us to pause and think about Jesus, and His life, and the effect of His life on our lives.

Unexpectedly, I remembered the incident in the living room of our old house so many years earlier. While I reconstructed the scene for the whole family, I knew that Joshua's recollection, like mine, was particularly vivid. "OK," I said. "You have the whole traumatic picture: Joshua has just tripped over the card table and is still on the floor, intensely aware of what he has done; the broken shards of the bowl are there beside him. I am, as you no doubt recall, furious. Now, with this in mind, I want you to imagine something else. There is a knock on the door.

May the humility
of the shepherds,
the perseverance
of the wise men,
the joy of the angels,
and the peace of
the Christ-child
be God's gift to you
this Christmas time
and always ✣

We open it. Imagine Jesus Himself standing there, patiently, expectantly. (He did drop in on people when He lived here. He has dropped in on us.) He walks into the room. He looks at us and, of course, is instantly aware of everything going on.

He bends down close to Joshua, gives him a brief reassuring hug, then very carefully picks up all of the fragments of the broken bowl. At His touch it is whole again. He hands it back to us. We look at Him. He looks at us. We look at the bowl, not a single crack or chip, half-full of water, red blossoms floating, carp swimming. His touch has made it better than new. This is His plan for us, as well. He intends to make us better than new.

WE NEED TO HAVE PEOPLE WHO MEAN SOMETHING TO US · PEOPLE WE CAN TURN TO
So that being with them is like coming home

Home

Epilogue

I WAS TRAVELING to my friends' home in Princeton, New Jersey, hoping to arrive in time for dinner. I was not sure of the way, so after a few false turns I was relieved and grateful when I saw the sign in my headlights, "Princeton. 15 miles."

I sometimes think these pictures can be like that. Their chief purpose is extrinsic, a purpose that, like the road sign, lies in pointing — or suggesting — a direction, a goal. What is important, ultimately, is not the sign — or the picture. What is important is being with my friends, breaking bread, finding my way along a dark road, getting home.